Meals Around the World

Meals in Vietnam

by R.J. Bailey

Bullfrog
Books

Ideas for Parents and Teachers

Bullfrog Books let children practice reading informational text at the earliest reading levels. Repetition, familiar words, and photo labels support early readers.

Before Reading

- Discuss the cover photo. What does it tell them?
- Look at the picture glossary together. Read and discuss the words.

Read the Book

- "Walk" through the book and look at the photos. Let the child ask questions. Point out the photo labels.
- Read the book to the child, or have him or her read independently.

After Reading

- Prompt the child to think more. Ask: Have you ever eaten Vietnamese food? Were the flavors new to you? What did you like best?

Bullfrog Books are published by Jump!
5357 Penn Avenue South
Minneapolis, MN 55419
www.jumplibrary.com

Library of Congress Cataloging-in-Publication Data

Names: Bailey, R.J., author.
Title: Meals in Vietnam / by R.J. Bailey.
Description: Minneapolis, MN: Jump!, Inc. [2016]
Series: Meals around the world | Audience: Ages 5–8.
Audience: K to grade 3.
Includes bibliographical references and index.
Identifiers: LCCN 2016016353 (print)
LCCN 2016016802 (ebook)
ISBN 9781620313787 (hardcover: alk. paper)
ISBN 9781620314968 (pbk.)
ISBN 9781624964251 (ebook)
Subjects: LCSH: Food—Vietnam—Juvenile literature.
Cooking, Vietnamese—Juvenile literature.
Food habits—Vietnam—Juvenile literature.
Classification: LCC TX724.5.V5 B35 2016 (print)
LCC TX724.5.V5 (ebook) | DDC 394.1/209597—dc23
LC record available at https://lccn.loc.gov/2016016353

Editor: Jenny Fretland VanVoorst
Series Designer: Ellen Huber
Book Designer: Leah Sanders
Photo Researchers: Leah Sanders, Kirsten Chang

Photo Credits: All photos by Shutterstock except:
Alamy, 5, 12, 16–17; Getty, 4, 8.

Printed in the United States of America at Corporate Graphics in North Mankato, Minnesota.

Table of Contents

Street Food

Kim is at work.

She sells fish.

She eats pho
for breakfast.

What is it? Soup!

It has noodles.

It has lime and mint.

It is time for lunch.

Duc eats rice noodles.

Hue eats noodles, too.
Where are they?
Inside the summer roll.

Mai buys rice.

She eats it with vegetables.

Yum!

11

Cai sells banh mi.

What are they? Sandwiches.

They have meat and vegetables.

We buy dinner.

We eat rice.

We eat meat.

Our food comes
with sauce.

It is made with fish.

We bought chuoi chien, too.

They are fried bananas.

They are sticky.
They are sweet.
Yum!

21

Make Chuoi Chien!

**Make this yummy dessert from Vietnam!
Be sure to get an adult to help.**

Ingredients:

- 6 tbsp flour
- 2 tbsp granulated sugar
- 1 egg, beaten
- ¼ cup milk
- 5 small, firm bananas
- ¼ cup peanut oil
- honey or powdered sugar

Directions:

❶ Mix together the flour, sugar, egg, and milk to make a smooth batter. Let the batter rest for one hour.

❷ Peel the bananas. Slice each banana in half lengthwise. Slice each half across into chunks about three inches long.

❸ Dip the banana pieces into the batter.

❹ Fry in hot oil for a few minutes or until golden brown.

❺ Drain on a wire rack or paper towel. Serve warm.

❻ Dip in honey or powdered sugar to make them sweeter.

❼ Enjoy!

Picture Glossary

banh mi
A sandwich made with crusty bread, meat, and vegetables.

pho
A soup made with broth, noodles, spices, meat, and vegetables.

chuoi chien
Fried bananas.

rice noodles
Noodles made from rice flour.

mint
A sweet, fresh herb (plant) used to make food taste good.

summer roll
A dish made of rice noodles, meat, and vegetables rolled up in rice paper.

Index

To Learn More

Learning more is as easy as 1, 2, 3.

1) Go to www.factsurfer.com

2) Enter "mealsinVietnam" into the search box.

3) Click the "Surf" button to see a list of websites.

With factsurfer.com, finding more information is just a click away.

WEATHER AND US

Rachel Chappell

FITZGERALD
BOOKS

Bethany, Missouri

Photo Credits:
Cover © Phaedra; Title Page © Glen Gaffney; Page 4 © Dubrovskiy Sergey Vladimirovic; Page 5 © Darren Baker;
Page 6 © Linda Armstrong; Pages 6-7 © Pichugin Dmitry; Page 8 © Michal Kolosowski; Page 9 © Mlenny;
Page 10 © Trout55; Page 11 © Frances Twitty; Page 14 © Jan Martin Will; Page 15 © Stas Volik; Page 17 ©
Lijuan Guo; Page 19 © Mike Graham; Page 21 © Juan Carlos Diaz P., Natalia V Guseva; Page 22 © Mypokcik

Cataloging-in-Publication Data

Chappell, Rachel M., 1978-
    Weather and us / Rachel Chappell. — 1st ed.
    p. cm. — (All about weather)

    Includes bibliographical references and index.
    Summary: Illustrations and text introduce various
types of weather and climate, including how it affects our
everyday decisions and how we feel.
    ISBN-13: 978-1-4242-1425-9 (lib. bdg. : alk. paper)
    ISBN-10: 1-4242-1425-4 (lib. bdg. : alk. paper)
    ISBN-13: 978-1-4242-1515-7 (pbk. : alk. paper)
    ISBN-10: 1-4242-1515-3 (pbk. : alk. paper)

    1. Weather—Juvenile literature.
2. Climatology—Juvenile literature.
[1. Weather. 2. Climatology.]
I. Chappell, Rachel M., 1978- II. Title. III. Series.
    QC981.3.C43 2007
    551.5—dc22

First edition
© 2007 Fitzgerald Books
802 N. 41st Street, P.O. Box 505
Bethany, MO 64424, U.S.A.
Printed in China
Library of Congress Control Number: 2007900199

TABLE OF CONTENTS

WEATHER AROUND US

Weather is important to us because it helps us make decisions every day. It affects what clothes we choose to wear and the activities we do outside.

Weather also affects how we feel. If it is rainy and gray, we sometimes feel gloomy or sad. Other times, if the weather is bright and sunny, we are happy.

WHERE DOES WEATHER COME FROM?

Our weather is caused by two main things: the sun and moisture in the air. These two things form clouds, make rain, and cause wind to blow.

Weather depends on other things, too. One is how near or far mountains and bodies of water are. The weather on top of a mountain is different from the weather at the bottom. The weather near a large body of water is different from the weather inland.

HOW DOES WEATHER CHANGE?

Weather changes every day. The atmosphere, or layer of air above the Earth's surface, is where weather takes place. When things in the atmosphere like wind, clouds, and rain change, our weather changes.

Air masses are large pieces of air that move over the Earth's surface. If two air masses meet that have different characteristics, a **front** will form.

WIND

Wind is moving air across the Earth's surface. The atmosphere moves the Earth's temperatures from one place to another. This makes wind.

Strong winds during windstorms, hurricanes, and tornadoes can be very dangerous. Strong winds cause damage to trees, homes, and power lines.

CLiMATE

Climate is the weather pattern over a long amount of time. Average temperature and amount of precipitation influence climates.

Climate Zone
Average Temperature

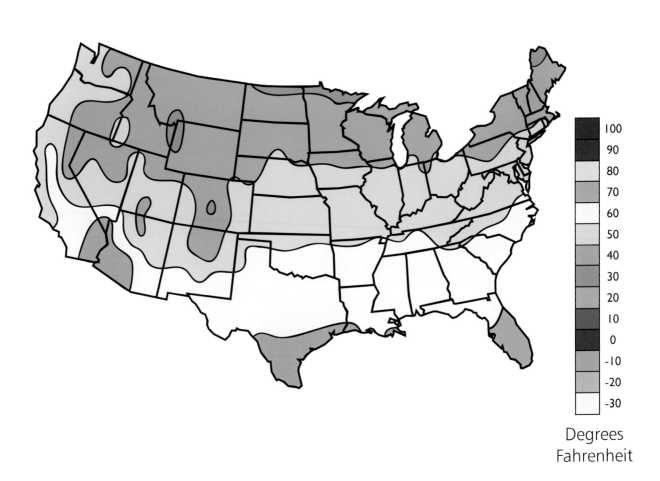

100
90
80
70
60
50
40
30
20
10
0
-10
-20
-30

Degrees
Fahrenheit

HOT AND COLD PLACES

Antarctica covers the southern end of our globe.
It is the coldest place on Earth.

Did you know that one-third of the Earth's land area is really dry desert? Many of these desert areas are near the **equator**.

WET AND DRY PLACES

The Amazon Rain Forest in South America is a tropical rain forest and gets nine feet of rain every year!

On America's northwest coast, there are temperate rain forests. **Temperate** rain forests are made up of evergreen conifers and usually have one long wet season.

Deserts are determined by how much rainfall they get each year. If an area gets less than 10 inches of rain a year, it is considered a desert climate.

Deserts are divided into two groups: the "hot" deserts and the "cold" deserts.

THE WEATHER AND US

What kind of climate do you live in? Is it dry and hot or wet and cool? Does your weather change often? Whether we like it or not, weather affects us.

21

Weather helps us decide if we should go on a picnic or stay inside. It helps us decide to wear a heavy coat or a light jacket. Weather also can make us happy, sad, or scared.

GLOSSARY

air masses (AER MASS uz) — great pieces of air in the atmosphere

climate (KLY mut) — the type of weather conditions that any place has over a long period of time

deserts (DEZZ urtz) — places where little or no rainfall occurs

equator (ee KWAY tur) — the imaginary line around Earth's middle

front (FRUHNT) — the boundary between two different air masses

temperate (TEM pur ut) — neither too hot nor too cold, moderate, mild

iNDEX

FURTHER READING

Green, Jen. *Changing Climate.* Chrysalis Education, 2003.
Sadler, Wendy. *Hot and Cold: Feel It!* Raintree, 2006.
Woodward, John. *Weather Watcher.* First American, 2006.

WEBSITES TO VISIT

Because Internet links change so often, Fitzgerald Books has developed an online list of websites related to the subject of this book. This site is updated regularly. Please use this link to access the list: www.fitzgeraldbookslinks.com/aaw/wu

ABOUT THE AUTHOR

Rachel Chappell is a teacher and author. She lives in Sarasota, Florida and enjoys skiing in the winter, shopping, and reading. Her family includes her husband, one son, and a dog named Sadie.